contents

Hickory-Smoked Barbecue Chicken Wings

MAKES 24 APPETIZERS

REFRESHING RECIPES

2	pounds chicken wings, tips removed, cut in half
3	teaspoons hickory flavor liquid smoke, divided
1	cup barbecue sauce
1	cup *Coca-Cola*®
⅓	cup honey
¼	cup ketchup
2	teaspoons spicy mustard
2	teaspoons hot pepper sauce
1	teaspoon Worcestershire sauce
¼	cup sliced green onions (optional)

1 Place chicken wings in large resealable food storage bag; add 2 teaspoons liquid smoke. Toss to coat. Refrigerate at least 1 hour to let flavors blend.

2 Preheat oven to 375°F. Spray 13×9-inch baking pan with nonstick cooking spray.

3 Combine barbecue sauce, *Coca-Cola*, honey, ketchup, mustard, hot pepper sauce, Worcestershire sauce and remaining 1 teaspoon liquid smoke in medium bowl; mix well. Pour sauce into prepared pan. Add chicken wings to pan; toss to coat.

4 Bake 35 to 40 minutes or until chicken is tender and no longer pink, basting occasionally with sauce and turning once.

5 Remove pan from oven and discard sauce, leaving just enough to coat wings. Set oven to broil and return wings to oven. Broil 3 to 4 minutes. Garnish with green onions, if desired, just before serving.

Coca-Cola® Chili

MAKES 4 TO 6 SERVINGS

1 pound ground beef

1 medium onion, chopped

4 stalks celery, chopped

1 can (about 15 ounces) tomato sauce

1 can (14½ ounces) beef broth

2 tablespoons chili powder

1 teaspoon garlic powder

1 teaspoon paprika

1 teaspoon ground cumin

1 can (15 ounces) kidney beans, drained

1 cup *Coca-Cola*®

1 teaspoon hot pepper sauce

Salt and black pepper

1 Spray 3-quart Dutch oven with nonstick cooking spray. Cook beef, onion and celery over medium-high heat until meat is browned and vegetables are tender. Drain excess fat.

2 Add tomato sauce, beef broth, chili powder, garlic powder, paprika and cumin to meat mixture; stir well. Bring to a boil over high heat. Reduce heat and let simmer, uncovered, 20 minutes; stirring occasionally.

3 Stir in beans, *Coca-Cola* and hot pepper sauce. Continue to simmer 10 to 15 minutes. Season to taste with salt and black pepper. Serve immediately. Garnish as desired.

Limelight Steak BBQ

2   large T-bone steaks (or other select cut suitable for barbecuing)

MARINADE:

2   teaspoons seasoning salt or steak seasoning

Fresh ground black pepper

3   tablespoons Worcestershire sauce

6   cloves fresh minced garlic

2   cans (24 ounces) *Coca-Cola*®

1 Using a fork, pierce each steak several times on both sides and place in a shallow glass baking pan. (Do not use stainless steel.)

2 Sprinkle steaks with seasoning salt and fresh ground black pepper. Pour Worcestershire sauce over steaks and add garlic. Turn steaks over to ensure they are well coated with seasonings.

3 Pour *Coca-Cola* over steaks to completely cover. Cover pan with plastic wrap. Refrigerate for 2 hours, turning steaks after the first hour. Discard marinade and barbecue steak to desired doneness.

REFRESHING RECIPES

Marinated Pork Tenderloin

MAKES 4 TO 6 SERVINGS

REFRESHING RECIPES

1	cup *Coca-Cola*®
¼	cup beef broth
2	tablespoons cider vinegar
1	tablespoon honey mustard
2	small Granny Smith apples, chopped
4	to 6 green onions, finely chopped
2	cloves garlic, minced
1	teaspoon ground cinnamon
½	teaspoon ground ginger
	Salt and black pepper
1	to 1½ pounds whole pork tenderloin

1 Combine *Coca-Cola*, beef broth, vinegar and mustard in large bowl; mix well. Add apples, onions, garlic, cinnamon, ginger, salt and black pepper to *Coca-Cola* mixture; mix well.

2 Place pork tenderloin in large plastic resealable food storage bag. Pour *Coca-Cola* mixture over pork, turning to coat. Seal bag and marinate in refrigerator at least 3 hours to let flavors blend, turning occasionally.

3 Preheat oven to 350°F. Remove pork from marinade, discard marinade. Place pork in roasting pan. Cook pork about 25 to 30 minutes or until internal temperature reaches 165°F when tested with meat thermometer inserted into thickest part of pork.

4 Remove pork from oven and transfer to cutting board. Let stand 10 to 15 minutes before carving. Internal temperature will continue to rise 5°F to 10°F during stand time. Serve with applesauce and your favorite side dishes.

Matchless Meatloaf

MAKES 4 TO 6 SERVINGS

1½	pounds ground beef
1½	cups fresh bread crumbs
¼	cup minced onion
2	tablespoons finely cut parsley
1	egg
½	cup *Coca-Cola*®
2	tablespoons ketchup
1½	tablespoons prepared mustard
1	teaspoon salt
½	teaspoon basil leaves
⅛	teaspoon black pepper

1 In bowl, break up meat with fork; add crumbs, onion and parsley, mixing well. Beat egg, mix remaining ingredients. Pour over meat. With fork, toss lightly to blend thoroughly. Mixture will be soft.

2 Turn into a 9×5×3-inch loaf pan. Bake at 350°F for 1 hour. Let set about 10 minutes before slicing.

Barbecued Ham

MAKES 4 TO 6 SERVINGS

2	pounds of ham (chipped)
1	cup ketchup
1	cup *Coca-Cola*®
1	chopped onion

1 At your local deli, purchase 2 pounds good quality ham and have it chipped.

2 In skillet, cook ketchup and *Coca-Cola* with onion. Cook slowly over medium heat. When it starts to thicken, add chipped ham and cook to desired consistency. Serve on hard rolls.

MATCHLESS MEATLOAF

Asian Beef Stir Fry

MAKES 4 SERVINGS

1½	pounds beef flank steak
1	can (12 ounces) *Coca-Cola*®
1	cup beef broth
3	tablespoons soy sauce
1	teaspoon sesame oil
2	cloves garlic, minced
3	tablespoons peanut oil, divided
1	yellow bell pepper, cut into thin strips
1	red bell pepper, cut into thin strips
4	green onions, sliced diagonally
1	cup water chestnuts
1	tablespoon cornstarch
2	cups hot cooked rice

1 Cut steak in half lengthwise, then crosswise into ⅛-inch strips. Place strips in large resealable food storage bag. Add *Coca-Cola*, beef broth, soy sauce, sesame oil and garlic; seal bag and turn to coat. Marinate at least 3 hours or overnight in refrigerator, turning occasionally.

2 Remove steak from bag; reserve half of marinade in medium bowl. Heat wok or skillet over high heat or until hot. Drizzle 2 tablespoons peanut oil into wok; heat 30 seconds. Add half of steak; stir-fry 2 minutes or until beef is browned and no longer pink. Repeat with remaining steak; set aside.

3 Reduce heat to medium high and add remaining 1 tablespoon peanut oil; heat 30 seconds. Add bell peppers, onions and water chestnuts; cook and stir 3 minutes or until vegetables are tender; remove and set aside.

4 Stir cornstarch into reserved marinade until smooth. Stir marinade into wok and boil 1 minute, stirring constantly. Return beef and vegetables to wok; cook 3 minutes, or until heated through. Serve over rice.

Beef Brisket

Center-cut beef brisket
1   **packet instant onion soup mix**
2   **(4-ounce) cans tomato sauce**
   Ground ginger
1   **bottle (2 liters) *Coca-Cola*®**
   Potatoes
   Carrots

1 In flat roasting pan, place beef brisket fat-side up.

2 Sprinkle onion soup mix on top of brisket, and pour 2 cans of tomato sauce on top. Sprinkle with ground ginger. Pour half of 2-liter bottle of *Coca-Cola* over meat.

3 Place whole potatoes and carrots around sides of pan. Add enough water to cover meat.

4 Place in 350°F oven for 3½ to 4 hours, occasionally spooning sauce over meat. If necessary, add a little more *Coca-Cola* or water to keep meat covered.

5 Meat is done when fork-tender. When finished, remove meat from pan and slice fat cap off top. Using an electric knife, carefully cut meat across grain into ¼-inch slices and place in casserole dish, covering with some of the sauce. Reserve some sauce to be used as gravy.

Casserole BBQ Chicken

MAKES 4 TO 6 SERVINGS

3	pounds cut-up chicken or chicken breasts, thighs and legs
⅓	cup flour
2	teaspoons salt
⅓	cup oil
½	cup onion, finely diced
½	cup celery, finely diced
½	cup green pepper, finely diced
1	cup ketchup
1	cup *Coca-Cola®**
2	tablespoons Worcestershire sauce
1	tablespoon salt
½	teaspoon hickory smoked salt
½	teaspoon dried basil leaves
½	teaspoon chili powder
⅛	teaspoon pepper

1 Rinse chicken pieces; pat dry. Coat chicken with flour and salt. Brown pieces on all sides in hot oil, then place pieces in a 3-quart casserole. (Discard drippings.)

2 Combine remaining ingredients, mixing well. Spoon sauce over chicken, covering all pieces. Cover casserole, bake at 350°F about 1¼ hours, or until chicken is fork-tender.

*To reduce foam for accurate measurement, use Coca-Cola at room temperature and stir rapidly.

Sweet and Spicy Shrimp Tacos with Mango Salsa

MAKES 6 SERVINGS

1½	pounds uncooked shrimp, peeled and deveined
1	teaspoon salt
1	teaspoon sugar
½	cup *Coca-Cola*®
⅓	cup chili sauce
2	tablespoons packed brown sugar
1	tablespoon lime juice
1	teaspoon hot pepper sauce
1	tablespoon chopped cilantro
6	lightly grilled flour tortillas
	Mango Salsa (recipe follows)

1 Place shrimp in medium bowl and sprinkle with salt and sugar. Stir to coat and refrigerate 30 minutes.

2 Meanwhile, heat *Coca-Cola*, chili sauce, brown sugar, lime juice and hot sauce in small skillet over medium heat until sauce begins to simmer and thicken. Remove from heat; stir in cilantro and set aside.

3 Cook shrimp in large skillet over medium-high heat 3 minutes or until shrimp are pink and opaque.

4 Drizzle sauce over cooked shrimp and serve in flour tortillas topped with Mango Salsa.

MANGO SALSA

2	mangoes, pitted and chopped
1	cucumber, peeled, seeded and chopped
1	red or yellow bell pepper, seeded and chopped
1	jalapeño pepper*, seeded and finely chopped
¼	cup diced red onion
1	clove garlic, minced

2	tablespoons chopped cilantro
1	tablespoon lime juice
1	tablespoon *Coca-Cola*®
	Salt and black pepper

Combine all ingredients in medium bowl and stir until well combined. Cover and refrigerate 1 to 4 hours before serving.

Jalapeño peppers can sting and irritate the skin, so wear rubber gloves when handling peppers and do not touch your eyes.

Sweet-Sour Cabbage

1½   pounds red or green cabbage
2   medium apples
½   cup *Coca-Cola*®*
2   tablespoons vinegar
2   tablespoons brown sugar
2   tablespoons bacon drippings
1   teaspoon salt
½   to 1 teaspoon caraway seeds

1 Coarsely shred or cut cabbage (should measure 3 cups).

2 Core and dice unpeeled apples. In pan, toss together cabbage, apples and all remaining ingredients.

3 Cover; simmer until cabbage is tender, about 25 minutes. Stir occasionally. Serve.

*To reduce foam for accurate measurement, use Coca-Cola at room temperature and stir rapidly.

REFRESHING RECIPES

Uncle Joe's Baked Beans

MAKES 4 SERVINGS

8	slices bacon, cut into ½-inch pieces
1	medium onion, chopped
1	can (12 ounces) *Coca-Cola*®
1	can (6 ounces) tomato paste
1	tablespoon Dijon mustard
1	teaspoon hot pepper sauce
1	can (15¼ ounces) kidney beans, drained
1	can (15 ounces) pinto beans, drained
2	cans (8 ounces each) crushed pineapple, drained

1 Cook bacon and onion over medium-high heat in large skillet until bacon is browned and crispy. Drain fat; set aside.

2 Preheat oven to 375°F. Spray 11×7-inch baking dish with nonstick cooking spray.

3 Combine *Coca-Cola*, tomato paste, mustard and hot pepper sauce in large bowl; mix well. Add beans, pineapple and bacon mixture to *Coca-Cola* mixture; mix well. Transfer to prepared dish. Bake, uncovered, 20 to 25 minutes or until beans are hot and bubbly.

Tip Baked beans are a real crowd-pleaser! Serve this summer favorite alongside burgers at your next picnic, barbecue, or family gathering!

Creamy Caribbean Shrimp Salad

MAKES 4 SERVINGS

1	cup mayonnaise
¼	cup cocktail sauce
¼	cup *Coca-Cola®*
1	teaspoon lime juice
½	teaspoon salt
¼	teaspoon black pepper
1	pound shrimp, cooked and cleaned
1	package (10 ounces) prepared mixed salad greens
2	ripe mangoes, peeled, pitted and sliced
½	cup chopped walnuts

1 Combine mayonnaise, cocktail sauce, *Coca-Cola*, lime juice, salt and black pepper in small jar with tight-fitting lid. Shake well. Refrigerate until ready to use.

2 Combine shrimp, salad greens, mangoes and walnuts in large bowl. Divide mixture onto plates. Drizzle dressing over salads.

Tip **The unique flavors of this salad make it an out-of-the-ordinary treat for your next gathering. For an extra special summer flavor, try grilling the shrimp before adding it to the salad.**

Brazilian Iced Chocolate

MAKES 4 TO 6 SERVINGS

2	squares (1 ounce each) unsweetened chocolate
¼	cup sugar
1	cup double strength hot coffee
2½	cups milk
1½	cups *Coca-Cola*®
	Ice cream or whipped cream

1 Melt chocolate in top of double boiler over hot water. Stir in sugar. Gradually stir in hot coffee, mixing thoroughly.

2 Add milk and continue cooking until all particles of chocolate are dissolved and mixture is smooth, about 10 minutes. Pour into jar, cover and chill. When ready to serve, stir in chilled *Coca-Cola*. Serve over ice cubes in tall glasses. Top with whipped cream or ice cream.

Tip **To put a twist on this tasty dessert, try it with different flavors of ice cream, chopped nuts, or caramel sauce.**

Chocolate Coca-Cola® Cake with Chocolate Cream Cheese Frosting

MAKES 1 CAKE

1 box (18¼ ounces) chocolate cake mix
1 cup *Coca-Cola®*
¼ cup water
½ cup oil
3 eggs
Chocolate Cream Cheese Frosting (recipe follows)

CHOCOLATE CREAM CHEESE FROSTING

1 package (8 ounces) cream cheese, softened
½ cup (1 stick) butter, softened
1 teaspoon vanilla extract
4 cups powdered sugar, sifted
½ cup unsweetened cocoa powder

1 Preheat oven to 350°F. Grease 2 (8-inch) round cake pans; set aside.

2 Combine cake mix, *Coca-Cola*, water, oil and eggs in large bowl. Beat at low speed of electric mixer until blended; beat a medium speed 2 minutes. Divide batter between prepared pans.

3 Bake 30 to 35 minutes or until toothpick inserted into centers of cakes comes out clean. Cool in pans on wire racks 10 minutes. Remove from pans to wire racks; cool completely.

4 Meanwhile, prepare Chocolate Cream Cheese Frosting. Combine sifted powdered sugar and cocoa in large bowl; set aside.

5 Beat cream cheese, butter and vanilla extract in large bowl until smooth. Gradually fold in powdered sugar and cocoa.

6 Place 1 cake layer on serving plate and frost top and sides with Chocolate Cream Cheese Frosting. Repeat with second layer.

Gingerbread Deluxe

MAKES 4 TO 6 SERVINGS

1	package (14 ounces) gingerbread mix
1	tablespoon instant coffee
1	tablespoon grated orange peel
¼	cup orange juice
¾	cup *Coca-Cola*®

1 Combine all ingredients. Beat vigorously with spoon until very well blended, about 1½ minutes.

2 Pour into 8×8×2-inch greased and floured pan. Bake in 350°F oven 30 to 35 minutes or until center springs back when lightly touched.

3 Cool 10 minutes; remove from pan and set on rack. Serve as a hot bread or as a dessert with whipped topping.

REFRESHING RECIPES